ESSENTIAL ELEMENTS
FOR BAND

COMPREHENSIVE BAND METHOD

TIM LAUTZENHEISER

JOHN•HIGGINS

CHARLES MENGHINI

PAUL LAVENDER

TOM C. RHODES

DON BIERSCHENK

To create an account, visit:
www.essentialelementsinteractive.com

Student Activation Code
E2BN-0705-3048-2088

ISBN 978-0-634-01287-7

HAL•LEONARD®
CORPORATION
7777 W. BLUEMOUND RD. P.O. BOX 13819 MILWAUKEE, WI 53213

REVIEW

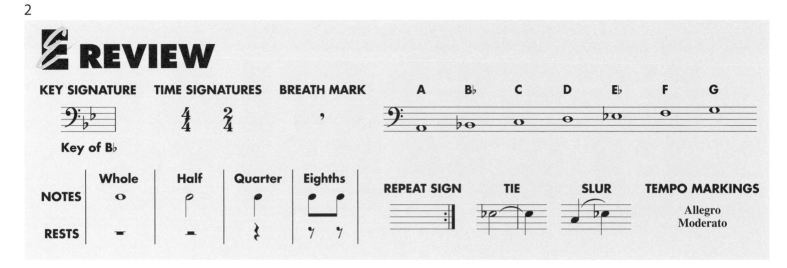

| KEY SIGNATURE | TIME SIGNATURES | BREATH MARK | A | B♭ | C | D | E♭ | F | G |

Key of B♭

| NOTES | Whole | Half | Quarter | Eighths | REPEAT SIGN | TIE | SLUR | TEMPO MARKINGS |
| RESTS | | | | | | | | Allegro Moderato |

1. TECHNIQUE TRAX

2. SHOO FLY

American Folk Song

Allegro

3. THAILAND LULLABY

Thai Folk Song

Moderato

4. SHEPHERD'S HEY

English Folk Song

Moderato

5. THE CRAWDAD SONG

American Folk Song

Allegro

REVIEW

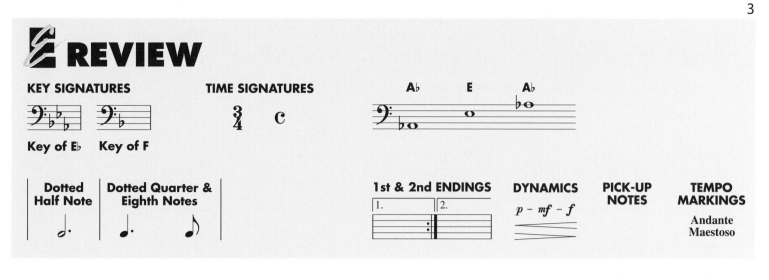

KEY SIGNATURES

Key of Eb · Key of F

TIME SIGNATURES

3/4 · c

Ab · E · Ab

Dotted Half Note · **Dotted Quarter & Eighth Notes**

1st & 2nd ENDINGS · **DYNAMICS** · **PICK-UP NOTES** · **TEMPO MARKINGS**

p – mf – f

Andante Maestoso

6. AMERICA/GOD SAVE THE QUEEN

Based on a Traditional Anthem

7. WEARING OF THE GREEN

Irish Folk Song

8. ROSES FROM THE SOUTH

Johann Strauss, Jr.

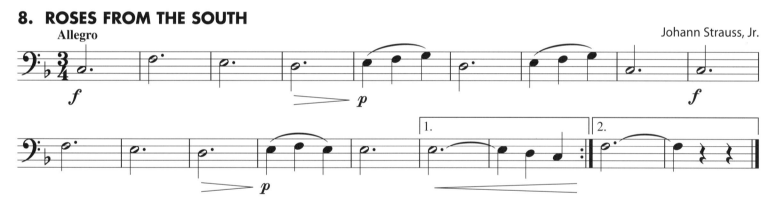

9. CRUISIN' THROUGH THE PARK

10. TRUMPET VOLUNTARY — Duet

Jeremiah Clarke

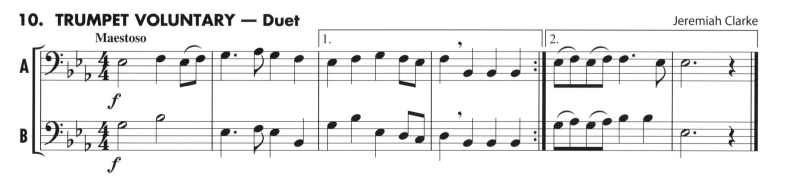

⚡ REVIEW

MULTIPLE MEASURE REST	ACCENT	FERMATA	D.C. al FINE
2	>	𝄐	

Eighth Note & Eighth Rest | **Eighth Rest & Eighth Note** | **Eighth Note & Dotted Quarter Note**

ENHARMONICS

A   B♭   C

C♯ D♭   F♯ G♭

11. CHROMA-ZONE

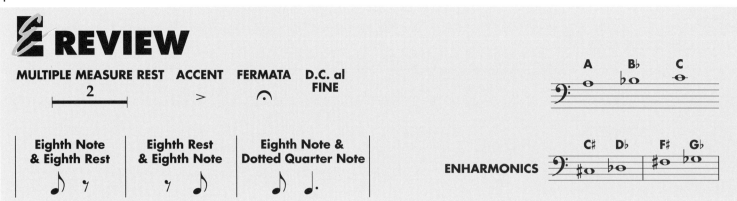

Fine

2

D.C. al Fine

12. BILLY BOY

American Folk Song

Moderato

13. TECHNIQUE TRAX

Allegro

1.   2.

14. SALSA SIESTA – Duet

Moderato

A

B

A

B

Staccato

Staccato notes are played lightly and with separation. They are marked with a dot above or below the note.

15. TREADING LIGHTLY

Tenuto

Tenuto notes are played smoothly and connected, holding each note until the next is played. They are marked with a straight line above or below the note.

16. SMOOTH MOVE

17. SHIFTING GEARS

English composer **Thomas Tallis** (1508–1585) served as a royal court composer for Kings Henry VIII and Edward VI, and Queens Mary and Elizabeth. During Tallis' lifetime, the artist Michaelangelo painted the Sistine Chapel.

Canons (one or more parts imitating the first part) were used in many forms by 16th century composers. A **Round** is a strict (or exact) canon which can be repeated any number of times without stopping. Play *Tallis Canon* as a 4-part round.

HISTORY

18. TALLIS CANON (Round)

Thomas Tallis

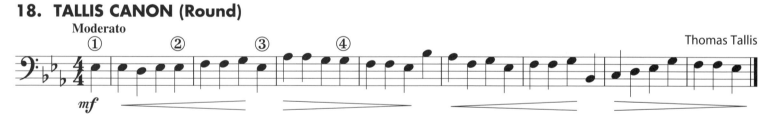

Sightreading

Sightreading means playing a musical piece for the first time. The key to sightreading success is to know what to look for *before* you play. Use the word **S-T-A-R-S** to remind yourself what to look for, and eventually your band will become sightreading STARS!

S — **Sharps or flats** in the key signature
T — **Time signature** and **tempo markings**
A — **Accidentals** not found in the key signature
R — **Rhythms**, silently counting the more difficult notes and rests
S — **Signs**, including dynamics, articulations, repeats and endings

19. SIGHTREADING CHALLENGE

DAILY WARM-UPS

WORK-OUTS FOR TONE & TECHNIQUE

20. TONE BUILDER

21. FLEXIBILITY STUDY

22. TECHNIQUE TRAX

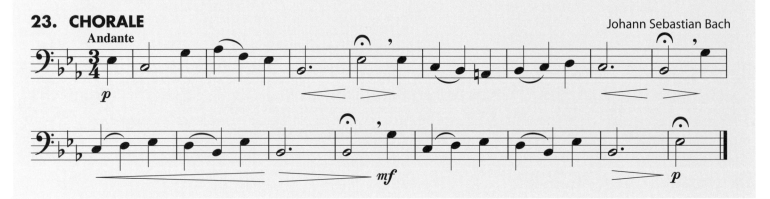

23. CHORALE

Johann Sebastian Bach

24. GRANDFATHER'S CLOCK

Henry C. Work

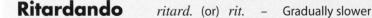

Ritardando   *ritard.* (or) *rit.* – Gradually slower

25. GLOW WORM

Paul Lincke

rit. ◁ Watch your director.

26. ALMA MATER – New Note
Practice long tones on all new notes.

A.C. Weekes, W.M. Smith, H.S. Thompson

The Scottish folk song *Loch Lomond* is credited to an anonymous soldier who was imprisoned and awaiting execution. In it he writes of his desire to return home to his family and the breathtaking beauty of Loch (Lake) Lomond, a lake in Scotland. Located in the southern highlands, the lake is almost entirely surrounded by hills. One of these is Ben Lomond, a peak 3,192 feet high.

HISTORY

27. LOCH LOMOND

Scottish Folk Song

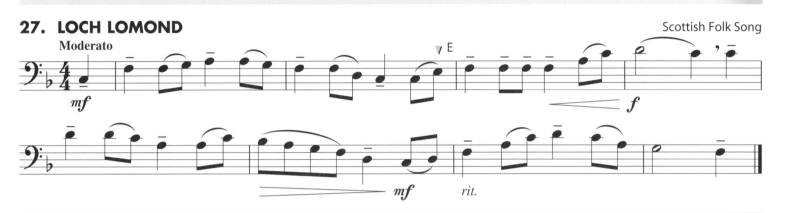

Key Changes

If a key signature changes during a piece of music, you will usually see a thin double bar line at the **key change**. You may also see natural signs reminding you to "cancel" previous sharps or flats. Keep playing, using the correct notes indicated in the *new* key signature.

THEORY

28. MOLLY MALONE

Irish Folk Song

Dynamics

cresc. = crescendo (or) ◁▷
decresc. = decrescendo (or) ▷◁

29. RISE AND FALL

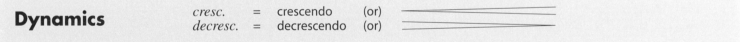

30. NO COMPARISON

31. SIGHTREADING CHALLENGE
Remember the S-T-A-R-S guidelines.

THEORY

₵ Time Signature
Cut Time (Alla Breve)

𝄢 ₵ or 𝄢 2/2 = **2 beats** per measure
= **Half** note gets one beat

o = 2 beats
♩ = 1 beat
♪ = ½ beat

32. RHYTHM RAP *Clap the rhythm while counting and tapping.*

Clap

1 & 2 & 1 & 2 & 1 & 2 & 1 & 2 & 1 & 2 & 1 & 2 & 1 & 2 & 1 & 2 &

33. A CUT ABOVE

1 & 2 & 1 & 2 & 1 & 2 & 1 & 2 & 1 & 2 & 1 & 2 & 1 & 2 & 1 & 2 &

34. TWO-FOUR YANKEE DOODLE

Moderato

American Folk Song

mf

35. CUT TIME YANKEE DOODLE

Moderato

American Folk Song

mf

36. MARIANNE

Moderato

Jamaican Folk Song

1.

2.

p cresc.

f decresc.

p

37. THE VICTORS

March Tempo

Louis Elbel

f

Count ➤ 1 & 2 &

1.

2.

1 & 2 &

38. ESSENTIAL CREATIVITY *Write this example in cut time ₵ before playing.*

Allegro

f

Allegro

Dynamics *mp* — *mezzo piano (moderately soft)*   Use full breath support at all dynamic levels. *p* — *mp* — *mf* — *f*

Syncopation occurs when an accent or emphasis is given to a note that is not on a strong beat. This type of "off-beat" feel is common in many popular and classical styles.

THEORY

American composer **George M. Cohan** (1878–1942) was also a popular author, producer, director and performer. He helped develop a popular form of American musical theater now known as musical comedy. He is also considered to be one of the most famous composers of American patriotic songs, earning the Congressional Medal of Honor in 1917 for his song *Over There*. Many of his songs became morale boosters when the United States entered World War I in that same year.

HISTORY

43. ESSENTIAL ELEMENTS QUIZ – YOU'RE A GRAND OLD FLAG

Words and Music by George M. Cohan

THEORY

New Key Signature

This key signature indicates your **Key of C** (no sharps or flats).

44. KEY MOMENT – New Note

B

C Scale — B — *Arpeggio*

45. THE MINSTREL BOY

Irish Folk Song

Andante

mp

1. 2.

46. CLOSE CALL – New Note

B

1. 2.

△ B

47. VICTORY MARCH

M. J. Shea

March Tempo

f

1. 2.

THEORY

Cut Time Syncopation

Compare the notation of the melody below with *Victory March* above. Should they sound the same?

48. WINNING STREAK

M. J. Shea

March Tempo

f

1. 2.

49. SIGHTREADING CHALLENGE *Remember the S-T-A-R-S guidelines.*

Moderato

mp *mf*

mp

Sixteenth Notes

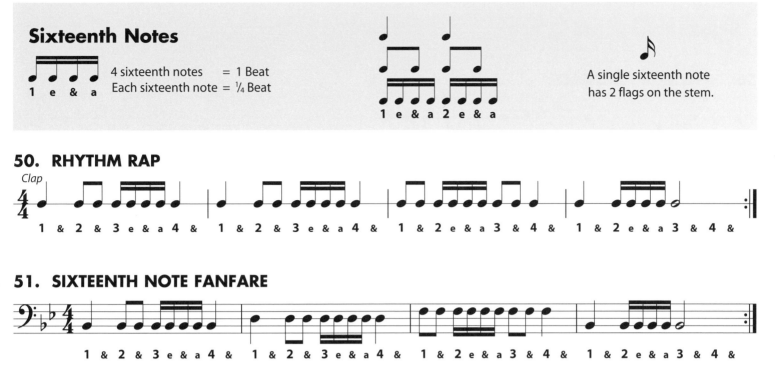

50. RHYTHM RAP

51. SIXTEENTH NOTE FANFARE

52. MOVING ALONG

53. BACK AND FORTH – Duet

54. COMIN' ROUND THE MOUNTAIN VARIATIONS

American Folk Song

55. ESSENTIAL ELEMENTS QUIZ

PERFORMANCE SPOTLIGHT

56. WARM-UP CHORALE

J. S. Bach/Arr. by John Higgins

57. THE THUNDERER – Band Arrangement

John Philip Sousa
Arr. by John Higgins

Reproduced by Permission of Boosey & Hawkes Music Publishers Ltd.

58. HILL AND GULLY RIDER – Band Arrangement

Jamaican Folk Song
Arr. by John Higgins

59. SHENANDOAH – Band Arrangement

American Folk Song
Arr. by John Higgins

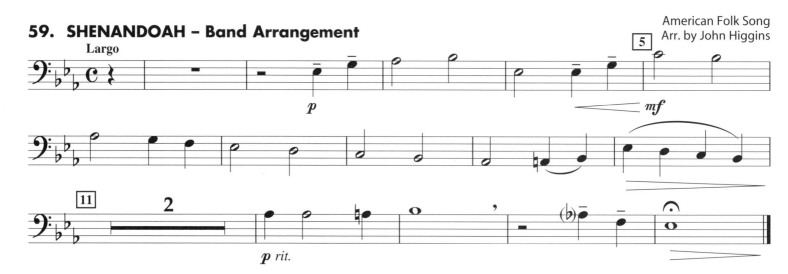

PERFORMANCE SPOTLIGHT

60. LAS MAÑANITAS – Band Arrangement

Mexican Folk Song
Arr. by John Higgins

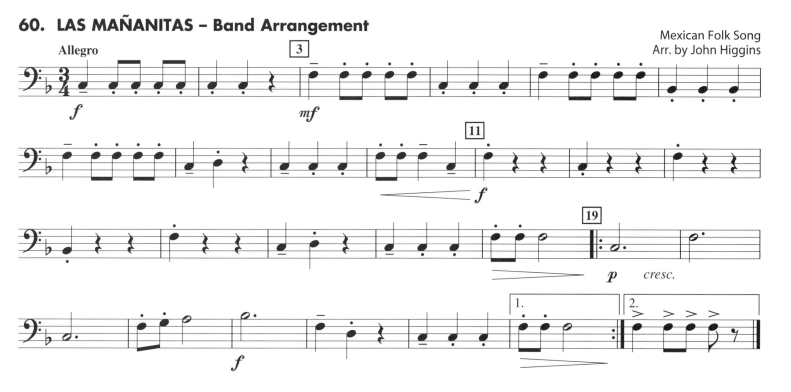

61. RONDEAU – Band Arrangement

Jean-Joseph Mouret
Arr. by John Higgins

D.S. al Fine–Go back to the sign (𝄋) and play until **Fine**. ▼

62. ROCK.COM – Encore Band Arrangement

John Higgins

69. RHYTHM RAP

70. RHYTHM ETUDE

71. BATTLE STATIONS

72. ENGLISH DANCE

73. BIG ROCK CANDY MOUNTAIN

American Folk Song

74. ESSENTIAL ELEMENTS QUIZ

Rallentando   *rall.* – Gradually slower (same as ritardando)

75. SIMPLE SONG – Duet

Watch your director

76. LINE DANCE

77. TECHNIQUE TRAX

△ *Keep 16ths steady*

78. THE GALWAY PIPER

Irish Reel

79. MANHATTAN BEACH MARCH

John Philip Sousa

80. SIGHTREADING CHALLENGE   *Remember the S-T-A-R-S guidelines.*

81. RHYTHM RAP
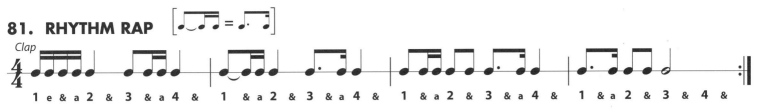

82. MARCHING ALONG

83. FANFARE FOR BAND – Trio

84. O TANNENBAUM
German Carol

85. S'VIVON
Traditional Hanukkah Song

86. GOOD KING WENCESLAS
English Carol

18

DAILY WARM-UPS
WORK-OUTS FOR TONE & TECHNIQUE

87. TONE BUILDER *Play at a very slow tempo.*

88. FLEXIBILITY STUDY

89. TECHNIQUE TRAX

90. CHORALE

Johann Sebastian Bach

HISTORY French composer **Georges Bizet** (1838–1875) entered the Paris Conservatory to study music when he was only ten years old. There he won many awards for voice, piano, organ, and composition. Bizet's best known composition is the opera *Carmen,* which was first performed in 1875. *Carmen* tells the story of a band of Gypsies, soldiers, smugglers, and outlaws. Originally criticized for its realism on stage, it was soon hailed as the most popular French opera ever written.

91. TOREADOR SONG (from CARMEN)

Georges Bizet

92. LA CUMPARSITA

G. Rodriguez

Enharmonics

93. THE YELLOW ROSE OF TEXAS *Check the key signature.*

American Folk Song

94. SCALE STUDY – New Note

E♭

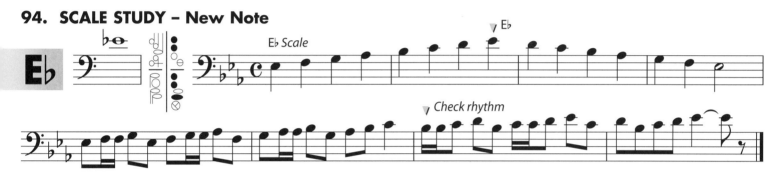

E♭ Scale

Check rhythm

Until 1974 Australia's official national anthem was *God Save The Queen.* A competition was held in 1973 to compose a new anthem, but none of the entries met with the judges' approval. Finally the government asked the public to vote, choosing from among Australia's 3 most popular patriotic songs. After easily defeating *Waltzing Matilda* and *God Save The Queen,* *Advance Australia Fair* was officially declared the national anthem of Australia on April 19, 1974.

HISTORY

95. ADVANCE AUSTRALIA FAIR

Peter Dodds McCormick

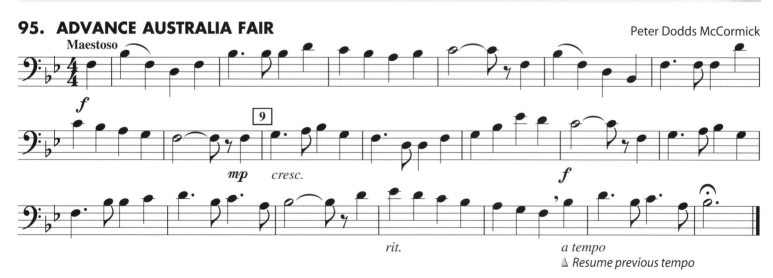

rit.   *a tempo*
△ *Resume previous tempo*

96. ESSENTIAL CREATIVITY

Arrange the melody of "America (My Country 'Tis Of Thee)" for your instrument. Write out the first line (6 measures).
Your first note is F. ADD: Key signature—key of F • Time signature—3/4 • Tempo and dynamic markings.

Play the completed line on your instrument to hear your own version.

97. AMERICAN PATROL

F. W. Meacham

98. ARIA (from MARRIAGE OF FIGARO)

Wolfgang Amadeus Mozart

HISTORY

American composer **John Philip Sousa** (1854–1932) was best known for his brilliant band marches. Sousa wrote 136 marches, including *The Stars and Stripes Forever*, which was declared the official march of the United States of America in 1987.

99. THE STARS AND STRIPES FOREVER

John Philip Sousa

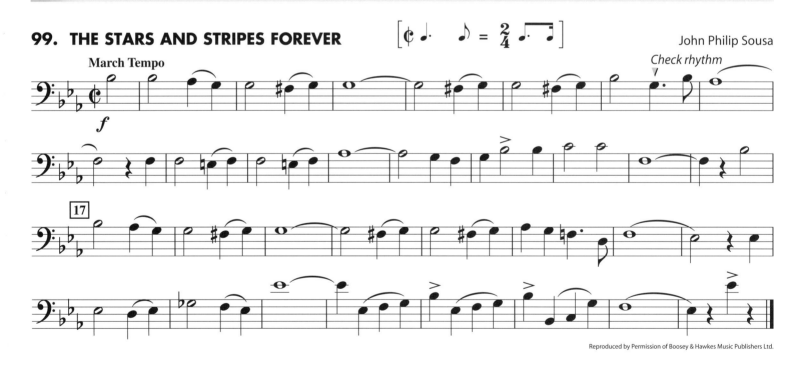

100. SIGHTREADING CHALLENGE *Remember the S-T-A-R-S guidelines.*

6/8 Time Signature

𝄢 **6/8**	= **6 beats** per measure	♪ = 1 beat	♩ = 2 beats
	= **Eighth** note gets one beat	♩. = 3 beats	𝅗𝅥. = 6 beats

6/8 time is usually played with a slight emphasis on the **1st** and **4th** beats of each measure. This divides the measure into 2 groups of 3 beats each. In faster music, these two primary beats will make the music feel like it's counted "in 2."

101. RHYTHM RAP *Clap the rhythm while counting and tapping.*

102. LAZY DAY

103. ROW YOUR BOAT

104. JOLLY GOOD FELLOW

> *Pick-up on beat 6*

105. CHANSON

French Folk Song

106. ESSENTIAL ELEMENTS QUIZ – WHEN JOHNNY COMES MARCHING HOME

American Folk Song

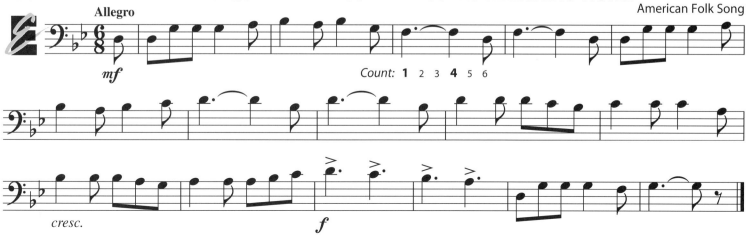

THEORY

More Enharmonics

Remember that notes which sound the same but have different letter names are called **enharmonics**. These are some common enharmonics that you'll use in the exercises below.

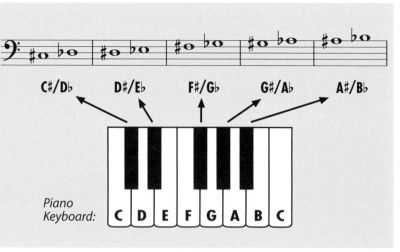

C#/Db   D#/Eb   F#/Gb   G#/Ab   A#/Bb

More Chromatics

The smallest distance between two notes is a half-step, and a scale made up of consecutive half-steps is a **chromatic scale**. These are usually written with **enharmonic** notes—sharps when going up and flats when going down.

Piano Keyboard: C D E F G A B C

107. CHROMATIC SCALE

Practice slowly until you are sure of all the fingerings.

△ Eb Enharmonic   △ Ab Enharmonic

108. TECHNIQUE TRAX

HISTORY

A **Habañera** is a Cuban dance and song form in slow 2/4 meter. It is named after the city of Havana, the capital of Cuba. Made popular in the New World in the early 19th Century, it was later carried over to Spain. There the rhythms of the Habañera were incorporated into many styles of Latin music. One of the most famous Habañeras is heard in Bizet's *Carmen*, written in 1875.

109. HABAÑERA (from CARMEN)

Andante   Georges Bizet

110. CHROMATIC CRESCENDO

Moderato

111. TURKISH MARCH (from THE RUINS OF ATHENS)
Ludwig van Beethoven

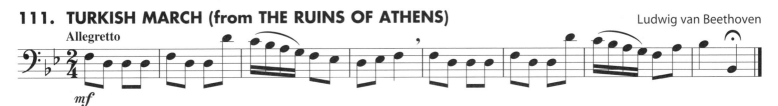

112. THE OVERLANDER
Australian Folk Song

113. STACCATO STUDY

114. YANKEE DOODLE DANDY
Words and Music by George M. Cohan

115. SIGHTREADING CHALLENGE
Remember the **S-T-A-R-S** guidelines:
S – Sharps or flats in the key signature, **T** – Time signature and tempos, **A** – Accidentals, **R** – Rhythm, **S** – Signs

24

Triplets

A **triplet** is a group of **3** notes played in the space of **2**. In $\frac{2}{4}$, $\frac{3}{4}$, or $\frac{4}{4}$ time , an eighth note triplet is spread evenly across one beat.

= 1 beat

1 trip-let 2 trip-let

116. RHYTHM RAP

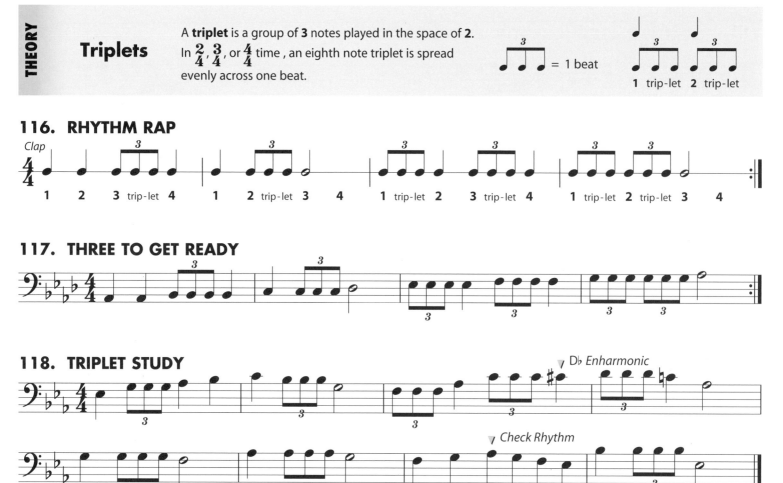

117. THREE TO GET READY

118. TRIPLET STUDY

119. MARCH (from THE NUTCRACKER) – Duet

Peter I. Tchaikovsky

120. ESSENTIAL ELEMENTS QUIZ – THEME FROM FAUST

Charles Gounod

121. SCALE STUDY – New Notes

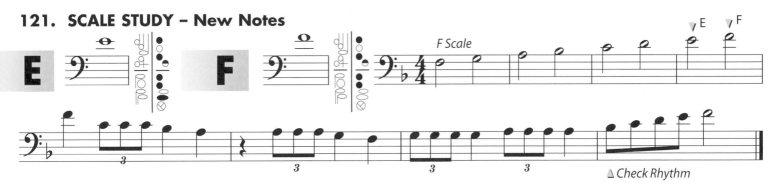

△ Check Rhythm

122. OVER THE RIVER AND THROUGH THE WOODS

American Folk Song

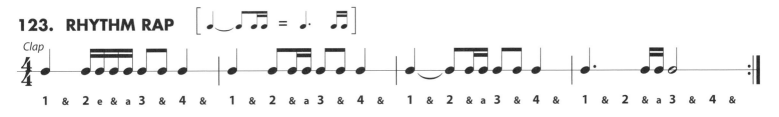

123. RHYTHM RAP

1 & 2 e & a 3 & 4 &   1 & 2 & a 3 & 4 &   1 & 2 & a 3 & 4 &   1 & 2 & a 3 & 4 &

124. ON THE MOVE

125. HIGHER GROUND

126. ESSENTIAL ELEMENTS QUIZ

The first known printing of the lyrics and music to **The Marines' Hymn** dates from August 1, 1918. An unknown author is believed to have taken the opening words of the song from the words on the Marine Corps flag, "From the halls of Montezuma to the shores of Tripoli." The music was taken from "Genevieve de Brabant," by the operetta composer Jacques Offenbach.

127. THE MARINES' HYMN

D.S. al Fine

Play until you see the **D.S. al Fine**. Then go back to the sign (𝄋) and play until the word **Fine**. **D.S.** is the abbreviation for **Dal Segno**, or "from the sign," and **Fine** means "the end."

128. D.S. MARCH

Accelerando

accel. – Gradually faster.

129. CAN-CAN

Jacques Offenbach

accel.

△ *Watch your director.*

130. TARANTELLA

Allegro

Italian Folk Song

f ▷ Pick-up

mf

HISTORY

The **waltz** is a dance in moderate 3/4 time which developed around 1800 from the Ländler, an Austrian peasant dance. Austrian composer **Johann Strauss, Jr.** (1825–1899) composed over 400 waltzes. These include such famous pieces as *The Blue Danube, Tales From the Vienna Woods* and *Emperor Waltz*.

131. EMPEROR WALTZ

Andantino ◁ *Tempo between Andante and Moderato.*

Johann Strauss, Jr.

mp

f

1.

2.

rit.

Legato Style 　　　*legato* – Played in a smooth, connected style.

---

132. ENGLISH DANCE – Duet

Johann Christian Bach

Andante

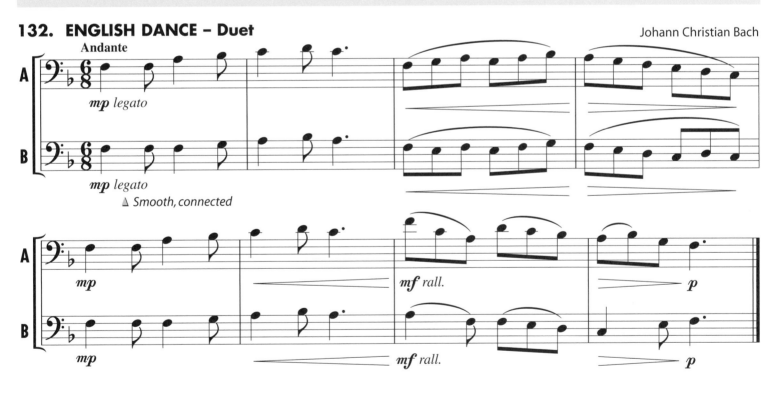

A

mp legato

B

mp legato

△ *Smooth, connected*

A

mp

mf rall.

p

B

mp

mf rall.

p

133. ESSENTIAL ELEMENTS QUIZ – BRITISH GRENADIERS

Traditional

Allegretto

mf

1.

2.

mp

cresc.

f

28

134. NASSAU BOUND

Bahamian Folk Song

Moderato

mf

Count ► **1 & 2 & 3 & 4 &**

135. UNFINISHED SYMPHONY THEME

Franz Schubert

Andante

mp legato

136. RHYTHM STUDY

3

Measure Repeat   ℔   Repeat the previous measure once for each **Measure Repeat** sign.

137. COUNTRY GARDENS

Allegretto

English Folk Song

mf

f

Measure Repeat

mf

rall.

138. JOSHUA

African-American Spiritual

Allegro

mf ——— *f*

mf ——— *f*

139. LISTEN TO THE MOCKINGBIRD

Alice Hawthorne

140. ANCHORS AWEIGH

Capt. A.H. Miles and C.A. Zimmerman

141. GREENSLEEVES

English Folk Song

142. THE LONG CLIMB

△ Measure Repeat

143. THE BLUE BELLS OF SCOTLAND

Scottish Folk Song

Major and Minor

THEORY

The scales you've already learned are called **Major** scales. They all follow the same pattern, with **half-steps** between notes 3–4 and between notes 7–8.

Natural Minor scales follow a different pattern, with **half-steps** between notes 2–3 and 5–6. The **G Minor** scale uses the same key signature as **B♭ Major.**

Another type of minor scale is called **Harmonic Minor,** which adds an accidental to raise the **7th** note by a half-step. Compare the scales on the right.

See page 37 for additional minor scales.

144. NATURAL MINOR SCALE – New Note

145. FINALE FROM "NEW WORLD SYMPHONY"

Antonin Dvořák

146. HARMONIC MINOR SCALE

147. HUNGARIAN DANCE NO. 5

Johannes Brahms

148. POMP AND CIRCUMSTANCE (LAND OF HOPE AND GLORY)

Edward Elgar

PERFORMANCE SPOTLIGHT

D.S. al Coda Play until you see the **D.S. al Coda**. Then go back to the sign (𝄋) and play until the **Coda Sign** ("To Coda" ⊕). Skip directly to the **Coda** and play until the end.

149. SIMPLE GIFTS – Band Arrangement

Shaker Folk Song
Arr. by John Higgins

150. SEMPER FIDELIS – Band Arrangement

John Philip Sousa
Arr. by John Higgins

PERFORMANCE SPOTLIGHT

151. DANNY BOY – Band Arrangement

Irish Folk Song
Arr. by John Higgins

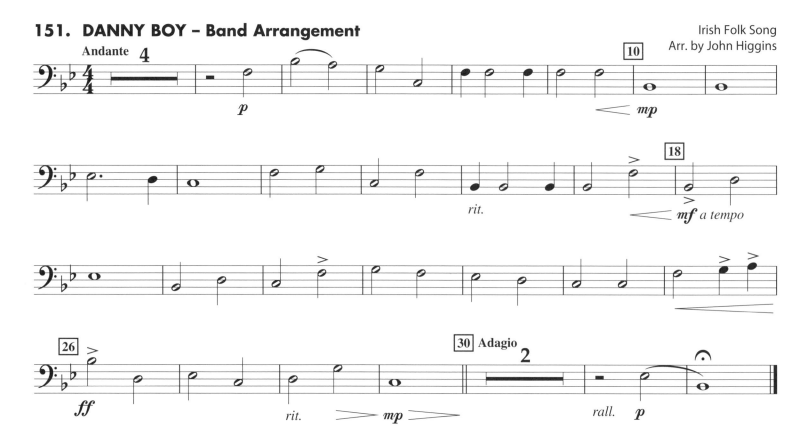

152. TAKE ME OUT TO THE BALL GAME – Band Arrangement

By Jack Norworth and Harry von Tilzer
Arr. by John Higgins

PERFORMANCE SPOTLIGHT

153. SERENGETI (AFRICAN RHAPSODY) – Band Arrangement

John Higgins

RUBANK® STUDIES

154. CHORALE

155. CHORALE

156. CHORALE

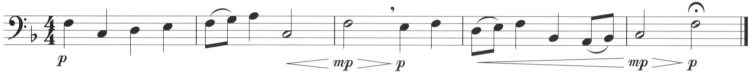

157. CHORALE

158. CHORALE

KEY OF Bb
159.

160.

161.

162.

RUBANK® STUDIES

KEY OF E♭

163.

164.

165.

166.

KEY OF F

167.

168.

169.

170.

RUBANK® STUDIES

KEY OF A♭

171.

172.

173.

174.

KEY OF C

175.

176.

177.

178.

RUBANK® STUDIES

KEY OF G MINOR

179.

180.

KEY OF C MINOR

181.

182.

KEY OF D MINOR

183.

184.

CHROMATIC SCALES

185.

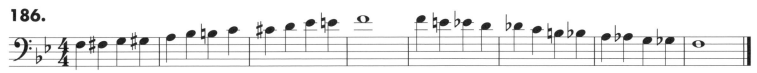

186.

INDIVIDUAL STUDY – Bassoon

187. LOW NOTE EXCURSION – New Note

CD Track 56

188. LOW ENHARMONIC STUDY – New Note

CD Track 57

189. BREATH CONTROL STUDY – New Note *Try both two and four measure phrases.*

CD Track 58

190. ARPEGGIO EXERCISE IN A♭ – New Note

CD Track 59

191. ARTICULATION ETUDE

CD Track 60

192. ARPEGGIO CHALLENGE

CD Track 61

INDIVIDUAL STUDY – Bassoon

193. TECHNIQUE STUDY #1
CD Track 62

194. TECHNIQUE STUDY #2
CD Track 63

195. CHROMATIC ETUDE #1
CD Track 64

196. CHROMATIC ETUDE #2
CD Track 65

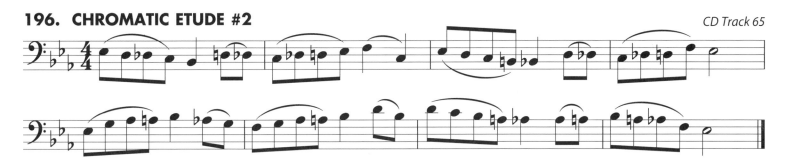

197. TRIPLET STUDY
CD Track 66

INDIVIDUAL STUDY - Bassoon

Solo with Piano Accompaniment

You can perform this solo with the piano accompaniment on the following page.

198. RONDO from "Suite in G" – Bassoon Solo *CD Track 67*

Allegro molto (♩ = 98)

Paul Koepke

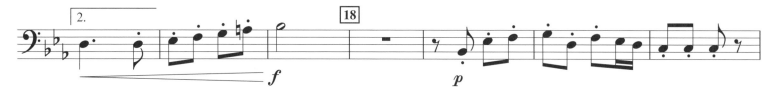

INDIVIDUAL STUDY – Bassoon

198. RONDO from "Suite in G" – Piano Accompaniment *CD Track 68*

Paul Koepke

RHYTHM STUDIES

RHYTHM STUDIES

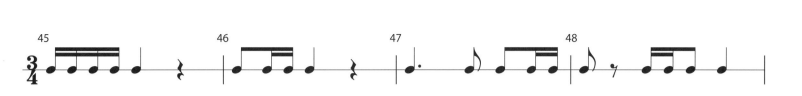

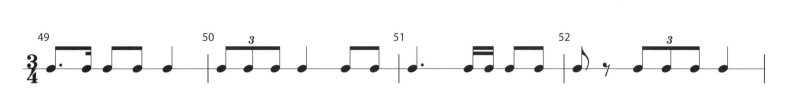

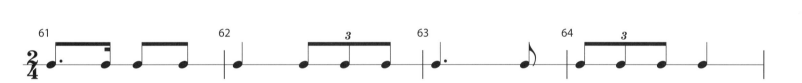

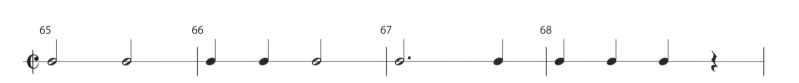

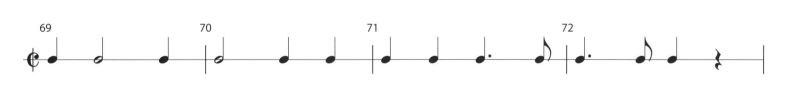

CREATING MUSIC

Theme and Variation

Theme and Variation is a technique used by composers and arrangers to create interesting musical ideas that are "varied" from an established melody, or "theme." Play the following theme and two variations to hear how the arranger has created new phrases based on the original melody.

1. THEME

"Simple Gifts"

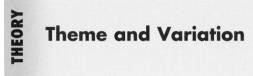

VARIATION 1 *Adding some notes • Changing some rhythms*

VARIATION 2 *Removing notes • Changing rhythms • Adding accents • Adding notes*

2. THEME AND YOUR VARIATION *Write your own variation of this theme. Use your instrument to hear and try different ideas.*

Theme

"Oh, Susanna"

Your Variation

Blues Improvisation

Improvisation using a **Blues Scale** is an important part of jazz and popular music. Musicians use combinations of these notes and various rhythms to create their own spontaneous solos over a 12 measure progression of chords.

Blues Scale

3. LET'S JAM *Use the indicated notes from the Blues Scale to create your own solo to play with the accompaniment (Line B).*

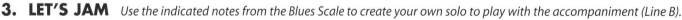
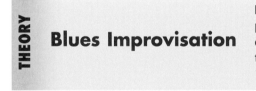

You can mark your progress through the book on this page. Fill in the stars as instructed by your band director.

ESSENTIAL
ELEMENTS

STAR ACHIEVER

NAME_____

MUSIC — AN ESSENTIAL ELEMENT OF LIFE

FINGERING CHART

Instrument Care Reminders

Before putting your instrument back in its case after playing, do the following:

- Carefully remove the reed and blow air through it. Return to reed case.
- Remove the bocal and blow air through the larger end to remove excess moisture.
- Take the instrument apart in the reverse order of assembly. Swab out each section with a cloth swab or cleaning rod. Drop the weight of the swab through each section and pull it through. Return each section to the correct spot in the case.

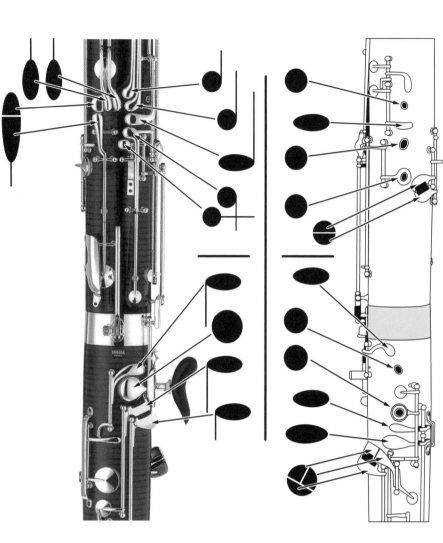

○ = Open
● = Pressed down
◒ = Half-hole covered
◓ = Quarter-hole open
◍ = Optional

The most common fingering appears first when two fingerings are shown.

Instrument courtesy of
Yamaha Corporation of America,
Band and Orchestral Division

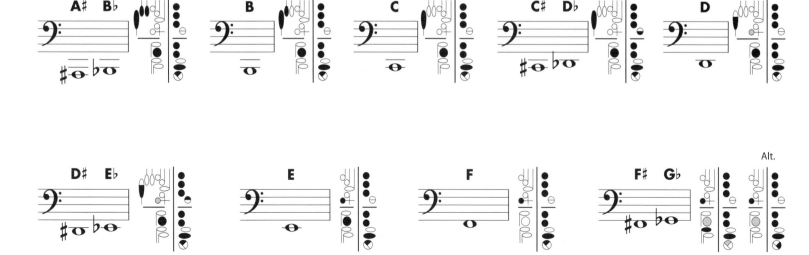

FINGERING CHART

BASSOON

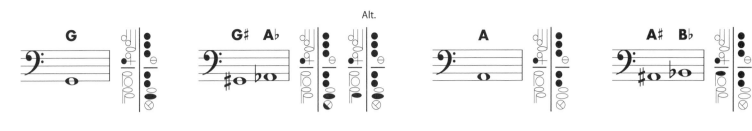

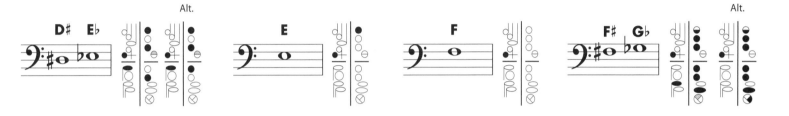

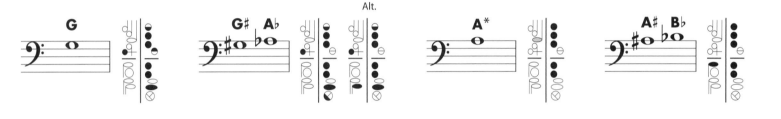

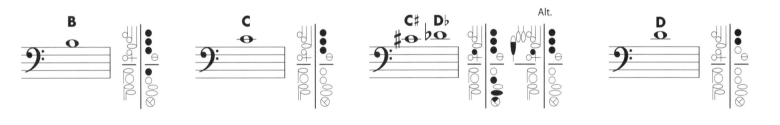

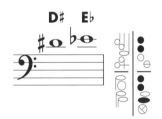

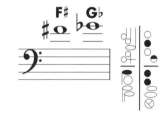

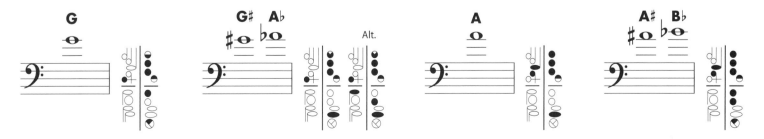

*The stability of this note can be improved by: 1) Venting the LH index finger ("quarter hole") or 2) Touching or "flicking" the high A key (shaded) at the beginning of the note.

REFERENCE INDEX